The Pink Panther™ Entertains

The PINK PANTHER™

Entertains

Food, Drink and Game Plans for Purrfect Parties

Lisa Skolnik and Adam Rocke
Illustrations by Shag

SURREY BOOKS
CHICAGO

THE PINK PANTHER™ ENTERTAINS is published by
Surrey Books, 230 E. Ohio St., Suite 120, Chicago, IL 60611.

Pink Panther illustrations by Shag
Designed and typeset by Joan Sommers Design, Chicago
Printed and bound in China by Imago

5 4 3 2 1

Library of Congress Cataloging-in-Publication Data
 Skolnik, Lisa.
 The Pink Panther entertains / Lisa Skolnik; Adam Rocke ; illustrated by Shag.
    p. cm.
  ISBN 1-57284-080-3
  1. Entertaining. 2. Parties. I. Rocke, Adam. II. Title.

TX731.S484 2006
642'.4—dc22
                                      2005024881

For free book catalog and prices on quantity purchases, contact
Surrey Books at the address above, or at www.surreybooks.com.
Distributed to the trade by Publishers Group West.

Parties

Purrfect Parties

When it comes to throwing a party, the best hosts don't take themselves too seriously—and the best parties don't come off without a hitch. But this kind of balance, which calls for confidence, an irreverent sense of humor, and the know-how to make lemons into lemonade, is rare. Fortunately, it can be honed, and there may be no better character suited to showing us how to sharpen these senses than one who embodies them himself—that infamous cool cat, the Pink Panther.

Part suave sophisticate and part sly prankster, the Pink Panther sports the kind of quick wit and hip charm we all want to possess. So with his sensibility in mind, we've planned eight parties that will let you embrace this outlook and shine, regardless of the limits you face or glitches that get in the way. If the Panther could talk, he'd undoubtedly say "cheers" to any party—so banish your fears and follow our step-by-step instructions to have a groovy time. . . the Pink Panther way.

How do you pull off a party?

The Pink Panther certainly knows how to party. But planning one is a whole different walk on the wild side.

There are plenty of pros who will give you their takes on the topic, but their advice always seems to boil down to the same old routine: culinary hotshots relying on recipes, party planners resorting to decorative "wow" tactics, and lifestyle gurus taking bits and pieces from both approaches.

All three strategies have merit—if you're after fabulous food, an incredible setting, or a perfectly coordinated affair. But frankly, none of them guarantees you or your guests a good time, which is, after all, the point of having a party. The Pink Panther, a quintessential good-time guy, knows that entertaining isn't about having the cleanest house, creating the most divine setting, or serving the most fabulous food. It's not about perfection, either, but about having an outrageously good time!

Nothing substitutes for making your guests feel wanted, welcome, and entertained. This is where the Panther Principles come in. They are based on the idea that having fun outweighs perfection. You'll find them placed throughout the book; follow them to a **P** (for Pink Panther, of course), or pick and choose the parts that work for you. Here's what to remember when you want to slink on the pink side.

1. Have a cool, simple game plan and follow it.
2. Don't worry about being interesting; just be interested in your guests.
3. Feel free to break the rules and invent new ones as needed.

Of course we realize that all this is easier said than done. Not all of us are instant V.I.P.s (Very Important Panthers). So for those who need a little instruction or a bit of inspiration, we've stacked the following pages with all the advice you need to succeed, from basic game plans and menus to down-and-dirty tricks.

Getting Started

Throwing a party, like solving a crime, calls for a strategy. You always need a game plan to de-mystify a process. But don't consult Inspector Clouseau, who would go overboard and bungle everything. Instead, break it down to the basics: who you want—or need—to invite; what kind of party or get-together to have; where to hold your shindig; when to have it; and how to pull it off. Here are the basics on each point:

WHO With his appetite for socialites and eccentrics, the Pink Panther knows intrinsically that you need all sorts of characters to keep things interesting. He's right! Bottom line: a good guest list is all about the mix. To insure a fun time, you need to bring together people from different walks of life; otherwise everyone will talk about the same old stuff—and that's boring. Invite guests of different ages and ethnic groups, with varied interests, political views, sexual orientations, and professions. Include lively types to counteract the reserved; outgoing souls to balance the bashful; and at least one screwball or outrageous type, if you know one. If not, you can make like the Pink Panther and handle that role yourself. For a sit-down dinner party, you'll need more of those perfect mixers who can talk to anyone; for a buffet you can get away with more quiet types. But follow the Panther and work your crowd, keeping his relaxed confidence and suave style in mind. Even when things go wrong for the Pink Panther, he tries to remain one cool cat.

WHAT Decide what kind of party you want to have—a night with your best friends, an intimate dinner for four, a casual brunch for eight, a patio party for a dozen, or a big, blowout cocktail bash. (You can guess what the Panther would choose!) Be strategic: you can turn a payback party for your pals into a fast-but-fabulous cocktail hour or short-but-sweet dessert to-do. That way, you only have to don your Panther persona for a limited time. Or you can turn a birthday into a wild and crazy game night. You might even put a hip spin on a familiar theme by giving a gambling bash a glitzy Monte Carlo theme the Pink Panther would love, or turning a holiday open house into a fantasy costume party à la the Pink Panther circa 1963. We're not talking about fastidiously coordinated motifs, but rather something to make the party fun and memorable. Whatever you choose to do, have an organizing principle that dictates everything from the duration of the event to what you'll serve. This will keep people from just sitting around and looking at each other, which would be anathema to our partying Panther.

WHERE Though the Pink Panther is hardly the kind of guy to be strategic about his pad, you must be. After all, you don't have Cato to serve everything and then clean up when the guests are gone. Don't use your whole home to have a party. Instead, set up zones to direct guests to food and drink and encourage them to mingle. If you have a small place, turn one bathroom or bedroom into the bar (set up drinks over the tub and stash ice in the sink; or move a bed to one side of the room and get out the card tables). If you have a larger place, set boundaries to confine the party to a fixed area. Otherwise people will wander all over the place instead of interacting with each other. Hide any messes behind closed doors.

WHEN This may seem to be the easiest part of the process. Trust us, it isn't. If there are certain people you want or need to have—like a Pink Panther type who's always the life of the party or a colleague you want to repay with a nice dinner— call them before you issue any other invitations and make sure they're free to come. If there are several people you simply have to include, it can get complicated, so leave yourself enough time to accommodate everyone's calendars.

HOW Although you can play the role of the cool hipster at the party, you must be organized beforehand. From the minute you set your date, make a checklist that enumerates every detail of the event. Issue invitations, and ask people to RSVP—it's the only way you'll know if they got the invitation and the only way to get an accurate body count. You'll need a final guest count to know how much food, liquor, equipment, and help you'll need. Make sure you have the right cookware to make everything and the dishes, utensils, and platters you'll need to serve it. Then make a master list of everything that needs to be done and by when. Call friends or even a rental company to round up anything you don't have, from folding tables and chairs to tableware, plus a rack if there are coats to hang in a foyer or outside hallway.

Figure out the "entertainment" for the night. Though it would be cool to have live music, if you are budget-challenged, be sure to figure out what music you're going to play on your stereo system. (The Pink Panther theme is a must at some point!) Then designate a friend to act as DJ so you don't have to change CDs and work the room at the same time.

Clean your place in advance, and Panther-proof it (translation: put away breakables; just imagine what a Panther-type on the loose can do to your favorite vases). Close the doors to any room you don't want guests to see (like a messy home office). Two days before the party, set out dishes, glasses, silverware, serving pieces, and vases. The day before the event, set out the CDs you're going to use for back-ground music; get flowers, especially for the powder room; and figure out what you're going to use to make every room in your place smell good (be it scented candles, air spray, or aromatherapy plug-ins). The day of your party, get everything done an hour or two before guests show up so you can relax. Once guests arrive, don't pull a Panther and bop all over the place; it is imperative that you greet them at the front door. Be warm and welcoming. Point them toward your delicious drinks and introduce them to your other groovy guests.

Party Basics

INVITATIONS Even the Pink Panther has to change his ways to throw a successful party, since it is critical to put aside your cool and be solicitous. You want bodies on hand, not no-shows. If it's a large bash, send out invitations between four and six weeks ahead; if it's more casual or intimate, issue invites by phone three to four weeks in advance. Don't count on email; it can get lost or derailed by a spam filter. Make your invitation noticeable—people still get tons of snail mail and you don't want your invite tossed. While you can get extravagant and quick-print them at a stationery store, it doesn't always take a lot of dough to make an eye-catching invitation. You can use great store-bought invites and make them look distinctive inside and out. Write the party details and address the envelopes in a bold color or thick ink, and use a fabulous sticker from a craft store on each one. Spiffy stamps from the post office help, too. "Regrets only" invitations can be lost in the mail, so insist on RSVPs via phone. It's the only way to tell if your invitation actually got there—and the best way to turn on the charm if someone you really want to come can't make it. Start practicing your powers of persuasion. If you have to, be as smooth and convincing as a dry martini.

SUPPLIES Give up the Panther bachelor pad shtick. We know it has the illusion of cool, but it pays to keep a party cupboard (or a few shelves in a closet) stocked with some basics so you're always ready for company. This can include wine and hard liquor, drink mixes, disposable glasses, cock-tail napkins, hors d'oeuvres plates, and simple or fun dry snack foods (be it mixed nuts or fancy crackers for cheese). Having it all in one spot means you can have anyone back to your pad for drinks at the drop of a hat. You'll know you have something to serve and won't have to go rooting around for the stuff at the last minute. When you have a party, buy more than you think you'll need to save yourself the embarrassment of running out of something. Use anything left over to stock this supply stash.

DRINKS No Cato of your own? Unless you plan on acting as a bartender all night or hiring one, keep the drinks easy and self-service. To do this, limit the options. Instead of an open bar, include a signature drink that you make ahead of time (pink martinis, anyone?). Keep this beverage in pitchers and serve it stylishly (like in martini glasses dipped in powdered sugar or flavored drinks paired with matching hard candies). If liquor mystifies you, opt for drink mixes (like cocktail infusions in different colors and flavors). And give routine drinks a touch of class by using attractive metal bins filled with ice to serve cans or bottles of soda, flavored waters, juices, or beer.

If you have the cash to hire a bartender, get one who is affable and outgoing rather than just poised and suave. The cool quotient is nice, but bartenders are potential icebreakers, and a gregarious soul will do more for the party mood than a debonair Panther type. Finding one is easier than you might suspect. Be on the prowl when you're out at a bar or another event; if you come across a great bartender, get his name and start a file. If you do hire a bartender, remember to tell him what to wear—maybe something groovy and noticeable instead of the routine white shirt, black pants, and tie. This is a stylish party, after all, so think Pink—in color and attitude!

DECORATIVE LIGHTING Think Pink and remember something the Panther already knows: your pad is a stage. It's so easy to give your place a certain kind of vibe by just varying the lighting. To make it soft and romantic, change harsh light bulbs for ones in soft peachy hues, or use clusters of votives or candles for illumination instead of overhead lights. To add glamour or drama, up-light the room by putting small can lamps on the floor (preferably where someone won't trip over them) and pointing them against a wall. For something over the top, get strobe lights or mirrored disco balls from party rental places. For an outdoor party, glam up a garden with torchieres, string lights, lanterns, and votives. Don't forget to illuminate pathways for safety with votives on the ground or string lights in bushes or trees.

MUSIC Just think of the slinky feeling you get from the Panther's suave signature strains. Music undeniably makes the mood, so match it to the occasion to convey the ambiance you desire. The tunes you would play for a relaxing dinner are different from those you'd use at a blowout birthday bash or chic cocktail party. If your budget is limited, a selection of CDs is fine, but make your choices in advance to keep the ambiance on track. Consider tying the music to the food, like playing salsa or bossa nova music to echo a Latin American or Mexican-inspired menu. Base your choices on your activities—use melodic, sexy music for pre-dinner mingling, quiet background music for dinner, and dance music after eating. Vocals aren't ideal during dinner since they conflict with conversation. Also, don't forget to turn the volume up or down as your home fills or empties with people. For a special surprise, hire a DJ or live musician for some part of the evening, following the same process you would use to hire a bartender.

TABLES Though the Pink Panther is hardly a detail-oriented type of guy, he is definitely clever enough to know that you have to set the stage for a special occasion. And interesting or hip, decorative touches on the table can go a long way when you have to do this. To make the table engaging, vary the textures, patterns, or colors of its coverings. But if you have an attractive wood table, consider leaving it bare. To dress a table, consider "wrapping" the top in a pretty or exotic paper, using a patterned bed sheet in lieu of a tablecloth, or piling on several funky cloths for a layered look.

For drama, use creative touches such as oversized crystal, masses of votives, or candles in attractive holders and glass goblets, containers, or bowls filled with fanciful objects such as flower petals, shells, stones, fresh or dried fruit, or anything that strikes your fancy and looks good. Don't use anything that obstructs guests' views of each other, like gigantic flower arrangements or towering candelabras; they can stifle the conversation. Be like the Panther: go for something suave and sophisticated, not big and bold. Keep the accessories on your table low to pull the focus down and keep things intimate. Think supper club chic. Bottom line: people should be able to look each other in the eye.

SERVING PIECES Dishes have to be attractive, but you don't have to use the fine china. Disposables are okay if they're pretty instead of tacky, but you can also mix and match the boldly patterned or brightly hued plastic or melamine dishes you can find at mass merchandisers and party stores. Or use screwball-chic dishes from the dollar store. Consider using different types of china and flatware together. Be creative with serving pieces. Line wire or straw baskets with pretty cloth napkins or tea towels and use them to serve dry things like munchies, fruits, and breads. Meats with juices can be served in large, low-slung (and far more slosh-proof) bowls instead of on platters. Or dish out cold soups in tea cups or pretty clear plastic cups, and hot soups or chili in mugs; this makes them appropriate as an appetizer or easier to serve at buffets.

FOOD Can you picture the Pink Panther slaving away over a stove? Never! It would crimp that supremely smooth style. If this is you, remember—you don't have to make everything yourself, or even anything at all. Do it the Panther way: order in all the food and make really great cocktails. Use something super-simple but fun for appetizers—like five different kinds of popcorn. Just one element that's over the top will make a party special, so stick to what you do well. If you don't cook, tell everyone to bring a certain dish and create an incredible setting. If you do cook, contrary to popular thought, a party is not the time to show off your sophisticated palate with exotic gourmet dishes. This is the time to serve the dishes that everyone recognizes and likes—those tried-and-true classics and old favorites. Food should also reflect the nature of the event (casual or

formal, sit-down or buffet, full-blown or restrained)
and the season of the year (light and cool in the
summer, warm and welcoming in the winter). But you
can add a kick to a standard dish by spicing it up with a
surprise ingredient (like little bowls of pungent cheeses
to top burgers) or serving it in a special way (put those
gourmet popcorns in fancy bowls). But one standard rule still applies for fancier occasions:
no bones on buffets. That's just uncool.

HELP No matter how good you are at
multi-tasking, you can't entertain a large
group of guests and work the party at the
same time. If you've invited a crowd or are
serving multiple courses or a big buffet
and don't have a Cato-type to call on, hire
help. Despite rumors to the contrary, good
help is neither hard to find nor unafford-
able. You can corral the neighbor's kid into
doing kitchen duty, post a note at a local
high school, or call culinary
colleges that may have stu-
dents looking for extra funds.
Once your helpers report for
work, tell them what you want and
when it should be done—from
hanging up coats or passing
hors d'oeuvres to serving food and

washing and drying dishes. For a large crowd, you'll need a bartender and somebody to serve food and help clean. What the help wears can be your choice, though it should be simple and classy—and match the bartender's attire if you're using one.

SEATING Picture the Pink Panther as a hot air balloon and your guests as those sandbags that anchor him. Like balloons, center-of-attention types need sandbags to ground them. So if you detest the notion of a seating plan, get over it. It's basic party-sense to seat several sandbags around your balloons since the discourse will directly impact the success of any sit-down meal. As host, you should always tell people where to sit, and make sure two balloons don't end up next to each other. Also no one sits next to their best friend or spouse—someone new is always more interesting. If you're having a small, intimate dinner party, direct people to their seats individually as you invite them to sit down. Use place cards with a larger group so you can get them seated as quickly as possible. To keep things interesting, mix things up by re-seating your guests for dessert and switching spots yourself so your guests don't feel slighted. Put the second seating on the inside or back of the place cards, and have the men get up and move.

WORKING THE PARTY The Panther may not be a natural when it comes to playing host, but he is a quick study—and here are his new rules. To pull off the event with flair, take charge. Be ready at least 15 minutes in advance; guests have been known to be early. Station yourself at the front door, greet people the minute they come in, and give them something to do immediately—whether it's telling them where to put their coats or pointing them in the direction of the bar and suggesting the house specialty. To ensure that guests interact with each other, introduce them to each other as they come in. Have a big basket in the front hall for guests to place their cell phones, beepers, and pagers so ringing noises won't spoil the evening. Also, collecting these items acts as an icebreaker. Once everybody arrives, slink your way into the thick of things and put all your new-found know-how to work. Your party is sure to swing, and your pals will anxiously await your next soirée. Most of all: remember to have fun!

Melting Pot

**Linger over the fondue
pot at this casual
sit-down dinner and get
reacquainted.**

MENU
(serves 6)

Cocktails
Hors d'oeuvres
Cheese Fondue
Beef and Chicken Fondue
Chocolate Fondue

Game Plan

gives you something
to do, so this is an ideal
time to include friends who
don't know each other very
well. Any more than six and
you'll need double fondue pots
and a second table, so keep that
in mind if you increase the number
of guests. For a larger to-do, have
guests change tables between
dinner and dessert so everyone
gets to talk to each other. Use
casual serving pieces, not
paper, as fondue has a high
moisture quotient that will
soften paper plates.

Dreyfuss on the Rocks

1 $^1/_2$ oz. Scotch

$^1/_4$–$^1/_2$ oz. Chambord

Old Fashioned; pour over ice, stir. Cherry garnish.

Nutty Inspector

1 $^1/_2$ oz. Frangelico

$^1/_2$ oz. amaretto

$^1/_2$ oz. white crème de cacao

Old Fashioned; shake with ice, strain over ice.

Hors d'oeuvres

You're about to embark on a long,
lingering meal. A few nibbles, such as
bowls of olives or nuts, or assorted cut
vegetables are all that's necessary until
everyone is present and you're ready to
"dip in." Put paper napkins in a pretty
basket next to the nibbles and a small
bowl for pits and shells if you
serve olives or pistachios.

Cheese Fondue

1 garlic clove, halved

$1^{1}/_{2}$ cups dry white wine

2 teaspoons kirsch, optional

8 ounces Emmental cheese, coarsely grated

8 ounces Gruyère cheese,
coarsely grated

2 tablespoons cornstarch

$^{1}/_{4}$ teaspoon ground nutmeg

Salt and white pepper, to taste

Dippers: cubed French bread, apple and pear slices, quartered roasted red potatoes, blanched broccoli or cauliflower florets,
sliced bell peppers

Rub inside of large saucepan with garlic. Add wine and kirsch to saucepan and heat just to simmering over medium heat. Toss cheese and cornstarch in bowl; gradually add mixture to saucepan and cook over medium-low heat, stirring constantly, until cheese is melted. Cook, stirring, over medium heat until thickened, about 5 minutes. Stir in nutmeg; season to taste with salt and pepper. Transfer to fondue pot and serve with Dippers.

Beef and Chicken Fondue

1½–2 pounds boneless beef sirloin steak,
cut into ¾-inch cubes

1½–2 pounds boneless, skinless chicken
breast, cut into ¾-inch cubes

large bottle vegetable or canola oil

Dipping sauces: sweet-sour,
sour cream-horseradish, ginger-Mandarin,
mustard, BBQ, Thai, etc.

*Arrange meats on platters. Add oil to fondue pot and
heat according to manufacturer's directions. Using
fondue forks, cook beef and chicken in hot oil to desired
doneness, allowing 1 to 2 minutes per piece.
Serve with dipping sauces.*

Wine or beer?

With cheese fondue
consider a crisp Pinot Blanc
from British Columbia,
Washington, Oregon or New
Zealand or a dry Riesling or
Gewürztraminer. Beer is an ideal
drink to pair with fondue, the darker
the better. Try an Irish stout, like
Guinness. If you're feeling adven-
turous, pour Black Velvets—
half Guinness, half
champagne.

Chocolate Fondue

$^1/_2$–$^3/_4$ cup whipping cream

16 ounces bittersweet or semisweet chocolate, chopped

2 tablespoons Frangelico or Amaretto liqueur

Dippers: mini-biscotti, pretzels, cubed pound or sponge cake, banana pieces, strawberries, dried apricots, etc.

Heat $^1/_2$ cup cream in large saucepan over medium heat until simmering; remove from heat and add chocolate, stirring until melted. Stir in liqueur, and additional $^1/_4$ cup cream if desired for consistency. Transfer to fondue pot and serve with Dippers.

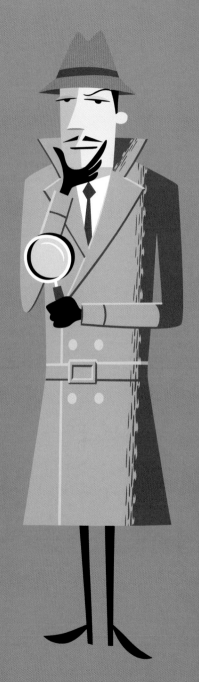

Pink Potluck

For any number of guests. Give a traditional potluck a little punch by asking everyone to bring their contributions in pink serving pieces.

Pitcher-Perfect Cocktails

Although cocktails prepared "en masse" in a pitcher or carafe usually don't taste as good as those prepared individually, some will work in circumstances where quantity is a requisite. Most martini-type drinks will get a thumbs-up from your tastebuds. Two drinks are stars: the Rusty Nail, which can be prepared "pitcher-style" and will taste as it should; and the Bloody Mary, an exception to the rule because a larger volume of ingredients actually enhances the taste.

Rusty Nail

2 oz. Scotch

1 oz. Drambuie

Serve in an Old Fashioned glass over ice. Multiply ingredients according to number of servings required.

Bloody Mary

1 $^1/_2$ oz. vodka

3 oz. tomato juice

$^1/_2$ oz. lemon juice

2–3 drops Tabasco sauce

2–3 drops Worcestershire sauce

1 dash each salt and pepper

Serve in a Collins glass over ice. Garnish with lemon/lime slice and/or celery stalk. Multiply ingredients according to number of servings required.

Appetizers

Give purchased salsas, dips, and spreads a spin by adding extra ingredients. It not only gives them more flavor and texture, it makes them look "homemade."

Black bean salsa—add quartered cherry tomatoes, whole kernel corn, chopped mango and/or cilantro.

Tomato salsa—anything goes! Add fresh chopped red or yellow bell peppers, whole kernel corn, coarsely chopped black or pinto beans or finely chopped oregano.

Spinach dip—heft it up with more chopped onions, a few minced garlic cloves, chopped artichoke hearts and chopped red bell peppers.

Cheddar cheese spread—stir in chopped mango chutney and chopped toasted walnuts.

Game Plan

If you're not a chef, this is the ideal way to go for a dinner party. You supply the pad, make something super-simple, and act as host. You can make it as casual or fancy as you like. Use fun paper and plastic accessories, or bring out the china and crystal, but make sure you create a setting to match the mood. If it's informal, anything goes. If pink isn't your thing, consider another motif, like fall harvest, and ask everyone to bring their contribution in a serving dish that celebrates the season. Or select an ethnic theme, such as Italian or Mexican.

Salads

Scrumptious slaws: shredded green and red cabbage both come prepackaged. Mix the two colors together and add interesting ingredients and dressings for tasty new takes on the classic slaw. Consider ingredients such as toasted cashews, crisp chow mein noodles, Mandarin orange segments and sweet-sour dressing for an Asian version, poppy seeds and toasted slivered almonds. Serve blush wine vinaigrette for a new classic; or drained pineapple chunks, chopped mango or papaya, macadamia nuts and honey vinaigrette for a tropical twist.

Entrees

Doctor up something store-bought, like spit-roasted chickens cut up and topped with a bottled sweet-sour, hoisin, mustard BBQ or horseradish sauce. Pile the chicken pieces on a great-looking platter and sprinkle generously with chopped parsley or other favorite fresh herbs.

Or make something quick and easy like the vegetarian pasta or chili below.

Roasted Eggplant and Tomatoes with Ziti

(serves 12)

Olive oil cooking spray

3 medium eggplants, unpeeled,
cut lengthwise into $1/2$-inch strips

6–8 medium onions, cut into $1/2$-inch wedges

$1^1/2$ teaspoons dried thyme leaves

$1^1/2$ teaspoons dried marjoram leaves

$1^1/2$ teaspoons dried savory leaves

Salt and pepper, to taste

3 cans ($14^1/2$ ounces each) diced tomatoes
with roasted garlic

$1^1/2$ pounds ziti pasta, cooked, warm

*Spray aluminum roasting pans with cooking spray.
Cut eggplant slices into fourths; arrange in roasting pans with
onions. Spray vegetables with cooking spray; sprinkle with
herbs, salt, and pepper. Roast vegetables at 450 degrees for
25 minutes. Spoon tomatoes over vegetables, and roast
10 minutes longer or until eggplant is tender. Serve over ziti
with freshly grated Parmesan or pecorino cheese.*

Wines

For pasta, there's really no rule . . . you can't go wrong with Italian—a good chianti or a nice dry white like Orvieto or Pinot Grigio.

Very Best (and Easy!) Chili

(serves 12 to 16)

3 pounds ground beef

3 cans (15 ounces each) pinto beans,
rinsed, drained

2 cans (28 ounces each) diced tomatoes,
undrained

2 cups frozen whole kernel corn

2 cups chopped onions

1 cup chopped green pepper

$1/4$ cup taco seasoning mix

2 tablespoons ranch salad dressing mix

Salt and pepper, to taste

Sour cream, for garnish

*Brown beef in Dutch oven; drain fat. Add remaining
ingredients, except salt, pepper and sour cream and heat to
boiling. Reduce heat and simmer, covered, 20 minutes. Season
to taste with salt and pepper. Garnish with sour cream.*

Easy Desserts

Turn plain ice creams into divine desserts by topping them with unexpected combinations. A few examples:

Top coffee ice cream with toasted pecan halves and coffee liqueur.

Top French vanilla ice cream with sliced fresh strawberries and a drizzle of good balsamic vinegar.

Top mint-chocolate chip ice cream with crumbled chocolate cookies, chopped fresh mint and mint liqueur.

Top peach ice cream with granola, a drizzle of honey and peach liqueur.

Top any sorbet or sherbet with mixed fruit, a dollop of whipped cream and a sprig of mint.

Tip!

You have to give people who are bringing food a little direction. Assign dishes, or ask what they want to make, indicating how many people their dish should serve. Make sure to get your numbers in order; if you're having 30 people, have at least 3 entrees for 12, 3 salads for 12, etc. And don't forget to assign some of the drinks, as those costs can add up for large crowds.

Coo-some Two-somes

A romantic soirée for two couples to reconnect should involve something you can all do together—like cook!

MENU
(serves 4)

Cocktails
Roasted Red Pepper Soup
Mixed Greens with Goat's Cheese
and Raspberry Vinaigrette
Steak au Poivre Flambé
Chocolate Passion

Cupid's Arrow

2 oz. citrus-flavored vodka

1 oz. light rum

$^1/_2$ oz. bourbon

$1^1/_2$ oz. pineapple juice

2 oz. cranberry juice

Collins; shake with ice, strain over ice.
Cherry garnish.

I Pink I Love You

$1^1/_2$ oz. gin

$^3/_4$ oz. cherry brandy

3 oz. pink grapefruit juice

Old Fashioned; shake with ice,
strain over ice. Cherry garnish.

Love Potion #21

$1^1/_2$ oz. sloe gin

$^1/_2$ oz. white crème de cacao

1 egg white

1 tsp. lemon juice

1 tsp. raspberry syrup

Old Fashioned; shake with ice,
strain over ice.

Keep appetizers to a minimum because the food you're serving is filling. Serve bowls of assorted olives, squeezing fresh lemon over them and garnishing with grated lemon or orange peel.

Hors d'oeuvres

Roasted Red Pepper Soup

1 small onion, chopped

1 clove garlic, halved

2 tablespoons olive oil

1 jar (15 ounces) roasted red bell peppers, drained

1 cup tomato juice

1 can (14$^1/_2$ ounces) vegetable broth

$^1/_2$ teaspoon dried marjoram

Salt and pepper, to taste

Sour cream, for garnish

Sliced green onion with top,
for garnish

*Saute onion and garlic in oil in medium
saucepan until tender, 3 to 4 minutes.
Process onion mixture, bell peppers and
tomato juice in blender or food processor
until smooth; return to saucepan. Add
vegetable broth and marjoram and heat to
boiling. Reduce heat and simmer, covered,
15 minutes. Season to taste with salt and
pepper. Serve in bowls or mugs; garnish each
with sour cream and green onion.*

Game Plan

Serve comfort food that has a touch of sophistication with some dishes that can be prepared in advance. Fine china isn't necessary, but paper won't do either. You can use your every-day dishes, but dress the table up with linens, use cloth napkins, break out some candles and don't forget the flowers. You can eat things as they're finished and take a break before the next course, or eat the soup out of mugs and sit down for the main course. Chocolate is the only decadent way to end the meal—make your fudgiest brownie recipe, or purchase something sinful from your favorite bakery.

Mixed Greens with Goat's Cheese and Raspberry Vinaigrette

1 package (5 ounces) mixed baby greens

$^1/_2$ cup dried cranberries or cherries

$^1/_2$ cup pine nuts, toasted

$^1/_2$–$^3/_4$ cup raspberry vinaigrette

$^1/_2$ cup crumbled goat's cheese

Toss greens, cranberries and pine nuts with raspberry vinaigrette in salad bowl. Sprinkle with goat's cheese and toss gently.

Steak au Poivre Flambé

2 tablespoons crushed
black peppercorns

4 filet mignons (1 inch thick)

Salt, to taste

1/2 cup brandy

Sprinkle pepper over both sides of steaks and press in well with fingers; let stand at room temperature 30 minutes. Heat greased skillet over medium–high heat until hot; add steaks and cook, turning occasionally, until desired degree of doneness, about 10 minutes for medium–rare. Transfer steaks to a chafing dish and sprinkle lightly with salt.

Add brandy to skillet, scrape up brown bits and pour over steaks. Heat in chafing dish until bubbly; ignite with a match and spoon flames over steak. Serve when flames subside.

Wines

For steak, opt for a full-bodied but versatile red wine such as a Pinot Noir from California or Oregon. Great bottles can be found in the $18–$30 range.

Chocolate Passion

4 large chocolate brownies, cut into
heart shapes, if desired

2 cups dark chocolate ice cream

3/4 cup hot fudge sauce, warm

Toasted pecan halves, for garnish

*Arrange brownies on plates; top with scoops
of ice cream, hot fudge sauce, and pecans.*

Nitecap

French Midnight

2 oz. brandy

1/2 oz. crème de noyaux

1 tbsp. amaretto

Coffee

2 tbsp. cream

*Hot Mug; pour brandy and
liqueurs, fill with hot coffee,
add cream, stir. Whipped
cream garnish.*

A Purrfect High Tea

For girlfriends who need an afternoon to bond, a spiritual tea with pink food and drink can give new meaning to the British tradition of high tea—an affair with food you can make into an entire meal.

MENU
(serves 8)

Beverages

Tea Sandwiches: Salmon Mousse, Prosciutto Melon and Radish

Fruit Tray

Pink Panther Kisses

White Chocolate Peppermint Treats

Game Plan

Make all the food in advance, serve it buffet and lay out the bar with make-it-yourself drink instructions—write them on something pink, of course! That way you can enjoy the party too. Dress up the serving table in pink, right down to the plates (paper will do), and even ask guests to don pink. Plan a fun activity like a Switch 'n Swap, having everyone bring 3 good items of clothing they don't want anymore—toss them in a pile and the hostess "peddles" each piece, one at a time, to the crowd. Whoever wants each piece gets it unless there's a conflict; then all takers have to try the piece on and the audience votes on who looks best in it.

Cato's Tea

$3/4$ oz. sake

I tsp. dark crème de cacao

Hot tea

I tsp. honey

*Hot Mug; pour ingredients,
fill with tea, stir gently. Add honey.*

Gin is the perfect
"proper English" spirit
to serve at high tea.

Bombay Sapphire Sun Kissed

I orange wedge

I $1/2$ oz. Bombay gin

I oz. Cointreau

$1/2$ oz. dry vermouth

*Rocks; squeeze orange wedge and drop
into shaker, fill with ice, add ingredients,
shake vigorously, strain over ice.
Orange twist garnish.*

Salmon Mousse Tea Sandwiches

(16 sandwiches, 2 per person)

$^3/_4$ cup flaked, cooked and drained canned salmon

$^1/_2$ package (8-ounce size) cream cheese, softened

1 $^1/_2$ teaspoons fresh lemon juice

1 $^1/_2$ teaspoons prepared horseradish

2 ounces smoked salmon, cut
into 1-inch pieces

1 tablespoon chopped fresh dill or parsley

Salt and pepper, to taste

16 slices firm white bread

16 very thin slices cucumber

16 dill or parsley sprigs, for garnish

Process cooked salmon, cream cheese, lemon juice, and horseradish in a food processor until just smooth; add smoked salmon and chopped dill and process until smoked salmon is finely chopped. Season to taste with salt and pepper.

Using a 2 $^1/_2$-inch cutter, cut a circle from each slice of bread; toast circles lightly. Spread salmon mixture on bread circles; top with cucumber slices and garnish with dill sprigs.

Prosciutto Melon Tea Sandwiches

(24 sandwiches, 3 per person)

6 ounces thinly sliced prosciutto or smoked ham

16 slices firm white bread, lightly buttered

$^1/_4$ cantaloupe or honeydew melon, peeled, seeded, very thinly sliced

Paprika, as garnish

Arrange prosciutto on 8 slices buttered bread; top with melon slices and remaining bread. Cut crusts from bread and slice each sandwich into 3 long fingers. Dust tops of sandwiches with paprika.

Radish Tea Sandwiches

(16 sandwiches, 2 per person)

12 large radishes, divided

1 package (8 ounces) cream cheese, softened

1 tablespoon finely chopped parsley

2 tablespoons finely chopped chives or green onions

2–3 teaspoons fresh lemon juice

Salt and pepper, to taste

8 slices pumpernickel or rye bread, crusts removed, cut diagonally into halves, toasted

Shred 10 radishes onto plate; squeeze out excess liquid with paper towels. Mix cream cheese, shredded radish, herbs, and lemon juice; season to taste with salt and pepper. Spread cream cheese mixture on bread triangles; slice remaining 2 radishes and garnish sandwiches.

Fruit Tray

You will need 4 to 6 cups of fruit, arranged attractively on a platter. Select pink fruits, such as cubed watermelon, strawberries and raspberries; combine with green grapes, sliced kiwi or blueberries for a colorful contrast.

Pink Panther Kisses

(16 kisses, 2 per person)

4 large egg whites, room temperature

$^1/_4$ teaspoon cream of tartar

1 $^1/_3$ cups superfine or granulated sugar

2 teaspoons strawberry or peppermint extract

2—4 drops red food color

Beat egg whites in large bowl on medium speed until foamy. Add cream of tartar and beat on high speed to form soft peaks. Beat in sugar gradually, beating to stiff peaks, about 5 minutes. Beat in extract and food color. Drop mixture into 16 mounds on parchment-lined baking sheets. Bake at 200 degrees until meringues are dry and firm, about 1 hour. Cool meringues in oven with door closed, about 2 hours. (Meringues can be made several days in advance and stored in airtight containers at room temperature.)

White Chocolate Peppermint Treats

(24 treats, 3 per person)

1 (16 ounce) container white chocolate frosting

3/4 cup powdered sugar, sifted

1 teaspoon vanilla

1 cup crushed peppermint candies

Beat frosting, powdered sugar and vanilla in bowl until smooth. Form mixture into balls, using scant tablespoon of mixture for each. Refrigerate until slightly firm, about 30 minutes. Roll balls in crushed peppermint candies; refrigerate until serving time.

Tiki At Twilight

Turn your balcony, patio or yard into a Tiki haven, and serve a playful buffet for ten. Start at sundown and light a few Tiki torches to make it dazzle. If the weather doesn't cooperate, head indoors, preferably to a pine-paneled basement, if you have one.

MENU
(serves 10)

Cocktails
Island Shrimp Dip
Date and Pineapple Rumaki
Ka-Luau Pork with Mango Salsa
or Maui Chicken
Corn, Black Bean and Jicama Salad
Macadamia Rice
Tropical Fruit Mélange

Game Plan

Mai Tai

1 oz. light rum

$1/2$ oz. triple sec

$1/2$ oz. orgeat syrup

$1 1/2$ oz. sour mix

*Collins; shake with ice, strain over ice.
Cherry and orange slice garnish.*

Frozen Pink Panther

1 oz. strawberry schnapps

1 oz. banana liqueur

1 oz. Malibu rum

2 oz. orange juice

1/2 oz. grenadine

Crushed ice

*Cocktail; blend all ingredients until smooth.
Cherry garnish.*

Tropical Rainstorm

1 oz. Malibu rum

$1/2$ oz. lemon-flavored vodka

$1/2$ oz. sloe gin

1 oz. pineapple juice

1 oz. mango nectar

*Old Fashioned; shake with ice, strain over ice.
Cherry garnish.*

Pinkolada II

1 ½ oz. Cabaña Boy strawberry
banana rum

1 oz. cream of coconut

2–3 oz. pineapple chunks
(fresh or canned)

2–3 oz. pineapple juice

2 tbsp. strawberry syrup

1 tbsp. light cream

3 oz. crushed ice

Goblet; blend all ingredients until smooth. Strawberry garnish.

Treasure Chest

1 oz. Jamaican rum

1 oz. spiced rum

1 oz. vanilla rum

1/4 oz. orange curaçao

1/4 oz. peach brandy

1 tsp. lemon juice

2 oz. orange juice

2 oz. pineapple juice

Collins; shake with ice, pour over ice. Cherry garnish.

Island Shrimp Dip

1 package (8 ounces) small curd
cottage cheese

8 ounces cooked, peeled, deveined shrimp,
finely chopped

$1/2$ cup thinly sliced green onions and tops

1–2 teaspoons prepared horseradish

$1/2$ teaspoon salt

$1/4$ teaspoon pepper

2–4 tablespoons milk

Dippers: Assorted crackers, sliced zucchini,
baby carrots, celery sticks, broccoli florets

*Mix all ingredients, except Dippers, using enough milk to make
desired consistency; refrigerate 1 to 2 hours for flavors to blend.
Serve with Dippers.*

Keep in Mind

Ask guests to dress
the part—Hawaiian shirts
for guys and pareos for gals
are easy to rustle up. Put
baskets of leis and beads at the
door for guests to toss on when
they enter, and play Tiki tunes,
available anywhere that has
a large CD selection.

Date and Pineapple Rumaki

(40 rumaki, 4 per person)

40 wooden toothpicks

2 packages (8 ounces each) pitted dates

1 can (15 ounces) pineapple
tidbits, drained

$^1/_4$ cup (2 ounces) crumbled blue cheese

20 bacon slices (1 pound), cut in half

$^1/_2$ cup packed light brown sugar

*Soak toothpicks in water while preparing dates. Stuff each date
with a pineapple tidbit and scant $^1/_2$ teaspoon blue cheese
crumbles. Wrap dates in bacon slices and secure with wooden
picks. Roll rumaki in brown sugar to coat bacon; place in jelly
roll pan and broil, 6 inches from heat source, until bacon is
crisp, 5 to 6 minutes, turning occasionally. Drain on paper
towels; serve warm or room temperature.*

Ka-Luau Pork with Mango Salsa

1 boneless pork shoulder (5–6 pounds)

2 tablespoons paprika

2 teaspoons garlic salt

1 teaspoon pepper

1 jar (20 ounces) mango or other fruit salsa

Rub pork with combined seasonings; place in roasting pan and let stand 1 hour. Roast, uncovered, at 325 degrees until pork is tender enough to almost fall apart (meat thermometer will register 170 degrees), 3 ½ to 4 hours, turning meat over every hour. Tent meat with foil and let stand 20 to 30 minutes. Shred meat with 2 forks and arrange on platter; serve with mango chutney.

Try This!

Choose either the pork or chicken as an entree for this festive menu. Should you be ambitious and want to serve both, select chicken breasts that are smaller.

Maui Chicken

2 bottles (10 ounces each) Teriyaki sauce

$^1/_4$ cup canola oil

10 skinless chicken breast halves (8 ounces each)

1 jar (16 ounces) pineapple preserves

Chopped fresh mint, for garnish

Pour combined Teriyaki sauce and oil over chicken breasts in large glass baking dish; refrigerate, covered, 1 hour. Drain and discard marinade.

Grill chicken over hot coals until cooked, 10 to 15 minutes per side, depending upon thickness of chicken; turn chicken occasionally, basting with pineapple preserves. Arrange on serving platter; sprinkle with mint.

Corn, Black Bean and Jicama Salad

1 large jicama, peeled, cubed

2 cans (15 ounces each) black beans, rinsed, drained

1 package (16 ounces) whole kernel corn, thawed

2 medium red bell peppers, chopped

2 bunches green onions and tops, sliced

1–2 bunches cilantro, chopped

Salt, pepper and garlic powder, to taste

Fresh lime juice, to taste

Combine jicama, black beans, corn, bell peppers, green onions, and cilantro in salad bowl. Season to taste with salt, pepper and garlic powder; season to taste with lime juice.

Macadamia Rice

10 cups cooked long-grain rice, warm

1 cup toasted macadamia nuts or cashews

Mix rice and nuts in serving bowl.

Tropical Fruit Mélange

8 cups cubed tropical fruit (mango,
papaya, pineapple, banana, kiwi)

Honey

1 quart fruit sorbet
or sherbet

Toasted coconut,
for garnish

Arrange fruit in stemmed compotes or bowls;
drizzle each with honey. Top with scoops of sorbet
and sprinkle with coconut.

MENU

(serves 8)

Cocktails

Crostini with Olive Tapenade

Rosemary Pecans

Penne with Vodka Sauce and
Smoked Salmon

Baby Greens with Dried Cranberries,
Walnuts and Blue Cheese

Bacon-Wrapped
Beef Tenderloin

A Pink Tie Affair

Throw a suave, sit-down
dinner with a blush when you
want to impress your friends.
The recipes serve eight but can be
increased for two to four more
guests. More than 12 guests
will compromise the intimacy
of the affair.

Cosmopolitan

1 $\frac{1}{4}$ oz. citrus-flavored vodka

$\frac{1}{4}$ oz. triple sec (or Cointreau)

$\frac{1}{4}$ oz. lime juice

1 $\frac{1}{2}$–2 oz. cranberry juice

*Martini; shake with ice, strain.
Garnish with lime slice or lime twist.*

Pink Champagne Cocktail

Chilled Tattinger (or similar pink) champagne

1 sugar cube

Twist of lemon

Dash of bitters

*Champagne glass; add ingredients
to the glass, fill with champagne.*

Pink Daiquiri

2 oz. light rum

1 oz. lime juice

1 tbsp. maraschino liqueur

*Cocktail; shake with ice, strain.
Lime slice garnish.*

Game Plan

Prepare as much in advance as possible so you can enjoy your guests. Pull out the real stuff (china, silver and cloth napkins) if you have it; if not, consider buying economical versions for the occasion. Paper plates won't do, even for the hors d'oeuvres, though you can get away with classy paper cocktail napkins. This may be the time to splurge on a helper for the night so you can focus on your guests. Don't forget sexy music to match the mood, like Bossa Nova or Latin jazz, but keep the volume low.

Pink Martini

1 $\frac{1}{2}$ oz. gin

$\frac{1}{4}$–$\frac{1}{8}$ oz. dry vermouth

1 tbsp. grenadine

Martini; stir (or shake) with ice,
strain. Garnish with lemon twist.

Classic

1 $\frac{1}{2}$ oz. brandy

1 tbsp. Cointreau

1 tbsp. maraschino liqueur

1 tsp. lemon juice

Cocktail; shake with ice, strain.

P.I. Special

1 oz. cherry brandy

$\frac{3}{4}$ oz. Scotch

$\frac{3}{4}$ oz. sweet vermouth

$\frac{3}{4}$ oz. fresh orange juice

Cocktail; shake with ice, strain.

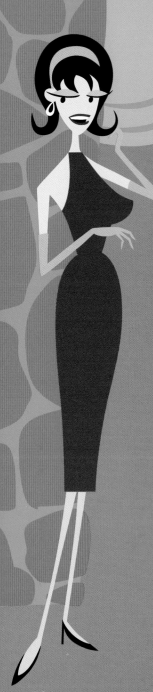

Bloody Simone

3 oz. tomato juice

$1/2$ oz. lemon juice

2–3 drops Tabasco sauce

2–3 drops Worcestershire sauce

I dash each salt and pepper

Collins; shake with ice, pour. Garnish with
lemon/lime slice and/or celery stalk.

Brandy Alexander

$1/2$ oz. white crème de cacao

$1/2$ oz. brandy

$1/2$ oz. heavy cream

Nutmeg

Cocktail (or Snifter); shake with ice,
strain over ice. Dust with nutmeg.

Pink Bombay

I oz. cherry brandy

I oz. dry vermouth

$1/2$ oz. sweet vermouth

I tsp. curaçao

Collins; shake with ice, strain over ice.

Crostini with Olive Tapenade

(24 crostini, 3 per person)

4 cloves garlic, divided

2 1/4 cups pitted Kalamata olives or other brine-cured olives

6 anchovy fillets

2 tablespoons drained capers

1 1/2 teaspoons chopped fresh thyme

1 1/2 teaspoons chopped fresh oregano

3 tablespoons fresh lemon juice

1/2 cup olive oil, divided

Pepper, to taste

1 French baguette, sliced into 24 rounds

Roasted red bell pepper strips, for garnish

Crumbled goat's cheese, for garnish

Wines

A medium-bodied red wine such as a pinot noir or a cabernet sauvignon is delicious with beef tenderloin. A small glass of vintage port or sauterne is perfect with dessert.

Process 2 cloves garlic, olives, anchovies, capers, thyme, and oregano in food processor until almost smooth; add lemon juice. Gradually add 6 tablespoons olive oil, processing until smooth; season to taste with pepper.

Arrange bread slices on 2 baking sheets; bake at 350 degrees until crisp and golden on both sides, about 15 minutes. Rub remaining 2 garlic cloves, halved, over 1 side of each crostini, then lightly brush with remaining 2 tablespoons olive oil.

Spoon olive tapenade on crostini; garnish with red pepper strips and goat's cheese.

Rosemary Pecans

(¼ cup per person)

2–3 tablespoons butter

2 cups pecan halves

1 tablespoon dried rosemary leaves

Salt, to taste

*Melt butter in medium saucepan; add pecans and
stir to coat. Cook over medium heat, stirring occasionally,
until beginning to brown, 3 to 4 minutes.
Sprinkle with rosemary and cook 1 minute longer;
season to taste with salt.*

Penne with Vodka Sauce and Smoked Salmon

16 ounces dried penne, cooked *al dente*, warm

1 jar (24 ounces) tomato-vodka sauce
(such as Emeril's) or favorite
pasta sauce, heated

8 ounces smoked salmon, cut into thin slices

Shaved Parmesan cheese, for garnish

Chopped parsley, for garnish

*Toss penne, tomato-vodka sauce, and smoked salmon
in serving bowl; sprinkle generously with
Parmesan cheese and parsley.*

Baby Greens with Dried Cranberries, Walnuts and Blue Cheese

8–10 ounces mesclun salad mix

$^1/_2$ cup dried cranberries or cherries

1 large tart or sweet apple, cubed

$^1/_2$ small red onion, thinly sliced

$^1/_2$–$^3/_4$ cup balsamic salad dressing

8 ounces blue cheese, crumbled

$^1/_2$ cup toasted or candied walnuts or pecans

Combine mesclun, cranberries, apple, and onion in salad bowl; toss with enough salad dressing to coat. Sprinkle with blue cheese and walnuts; toss gently.

Bacon-Wrapped Beef Tenderloin

1 beef tenderloin (about 4 pounds)

8 cloves garlic, quartered

1 tablespoon coarsely ground or cracked black pepper

1–1¹/₂ pounds sliced bacon

3 long rosemary sprigs

Cut ¹/₂-inch-deep slits in tenderloin with sharp knife and insert garlic into slits; rub all surfaces with pepper.

Arrange bacon slices on counter, overlapping slightly, to form a rectangle the same length as the tenderloin. Place 1 rosemary sprig in center of bacon rectangle and lay tenderloin on top; place remaining 2 rosemary sprigs on top of tenderloin. Wrap bacon around tenderloin to enclose it completely. Carefully turn over the tenderloin and place it in a roasting pan, with bacon ends on the bottom. (This can be done 1 day in advance; refrigerate, covered.)

Roast tenderloin, uncovered, at 450 degrees until meat thermometer inserted into center registers 140 degrees (rare), about 1 hour. Remove from oven; tent with foil and let stand 10 to 15 minutes before slicing.

Serve with broccoli or green beans, lightly blanched, and sauteed with a small amount of olive oil and garlic.

Dessert

You've concentrated your culinary efforts on an astounding meal—order dessert from a bakery. Offer a tempting sampling of miniature cream puffs, petits fours, cookies and chocolate truffles to assuage sweet cravings.

Pink Clinks

Break out the cocktail napkins and highball glasses, and relive the days when martinis were always consumed before dinner and stirred—not shaken. Complete the mood with slightly retro food that's polished and toothsome.

MENU
(serves 20)

Cocktails
Shrimp Bowl
Green Goddess Dip
Salmon Dip
Onion-Mustard Puffs
Mini-Quiches
Cheese and Fruit Platter

Vodka Gibson

1 $\frac{1}{2}$ oz. vodka

$\frac{1}{4}$ – $\frac{1}{8}$ oz. dry vermouth

Martini; stir with ice, strain.
Cocktail onion garnish.

Manhattan

1 $\frac{1}{2}$ oz. blended whiskey

$\frac{1}{2}$ oz. sweet vermouth

Cocktail; shake with ice, strain. Cherry garnish.

Pink Cooler

1 oz. Malibu rum

1 oz. Alize

6–8 oz. pink lemonade

Collins; shake with ice, strain over ice.
Lemon wedge and cherry garnish.

Pink Russian

1 oz. gin

1 oz. raspberry-flavored vodka

1 oz. white crème de cacao

1 tsp. raspberry sauce or raspberry puree

1 tsp. heavy cream

Cocktail; shake with ice, strain. Cherry garnish.

Shrimp Bowl

3–4 pounds large shrimp, cooked,
peeled with tails left on

Crushed ice

Parsley sprigs, for garnish

2 or 3 dipping sauces: cocktail sauce,
sweet-sour mustard sauce,
horseradish sauce

*Arrange shrimp over crushed ice in a large
bowl; garnish with parsley. Serve with
dipping sauces in small bowls.*

Green Goddess Dip

2 $^1/_2$ cups green goddess salad dressing

$^1/_4$ cup chopped parsley

$^1/_4$ cup snipped chives

$^1/_4$ cup chopped fresh tarragon

1 large shallot or $^1/_4$ small onion, chopped

Dippers: bread sticks, broccoli
florets, baby carrots, radishes, cherry
tomatoes, celery and zucchini sticks,
sweet potato slices

*Mix all ingredients, except Dippers;
refrigerate 2 to 3 hours for flavors to blend.
Serve in bowl with dippers.*

Game Plan

Have at least
two food stations,
as far away from each
other as possible to
encourage circulation and
keep everyone from crowding
in one spot. Pretty paper cocktail plates with matching paper
napkins are fine, but splurge on
real martini and highball glasses
(find them at outlet stores or mass
merchandisers, or rent them).
A bartender is also essential for
a party like this, or even two
depending on the size of the
crowd. Keep the music sexy and
suave, and adjust volume as the
crowd ebbs and flows (when
there are fewer people
present, turn the volume
up and vice versa).

Salmon Dip

2 packages (8 ounces each) whipped cream cheese

$1/4$–$1/3$ cup milk

4 ounces thinly sliced smoked salmon,
coarsely chopped

1 jar (2 ounces) red salmon caviar

2 tablespoons snipped chives

Pepper, to taste

Dippers: assorted crackers, cocktail rye bread,
cauliflower florets, carrot sticks, cucumber slices,
blanched sugar snap peas, asparagus spears

*Mix cream cheese and milk until smooth in bowl, using
enough milk for desired dipping consistency; mix in salmon,
caviar, and chives. Season to taste with pepper. Refrigerate
2 to 3 hours for flavors to blend. Serve in bowl with dippers.*

Onion-Mustard Puffs

1 loaf cocktail pumpernickel bread, toasted

1 cup mayonnaise

2–3 small sweet onions, thinly sliced

$1/2$ cup spicy or sweet mustard

Grated Parmesan cheese

Minced parsley, for garnish

*Spread bread slices lightly with mayonnaise. Top each with an
onion slice; spread lightly with mustard and more mayonnaise.
Sprinkle generously with Parmesan cheese and parsley. Broil 6
inches from heat source until puffed and golden, 3 to 4 minutes.*

Mini-Quiches

(40 quiches, 2 per person)

1 cup small-curd cottage cheese

$1/2$ cup (2 ounces) grated Parmesan cheese

2 tablespoons flour

$1/3$ cup finely chopped fresh spinach

$1/2$ teaspoon dried oregano

$1/2$ teaspoon dried thyme

Salt and white pepper, to taste

2 eggs, lightly beaten

40 frozen mini-fillo shells, thawed

Mix cottage cheese, Parmesan cheese, flour, spinach, oregano, and thyme. Season to taste with salt and white pepper. Stir in eggs. Arrange fillo shells on cookie sheet; fill with cheese mixture. Bake at 325 degress until puffed and beginning to brown on top, about 20 minutes.

Try This!

Don't forget two retro-favorites for your buffet table—deviled eggs and meatballs! Give deviled eggs a flavor tweak by adding crumbled crisp bacon and snipped chives to the yolk mixture. Serve purchased meatballs in a chafing dish, spiked with a spicy mustard-barbeque or sweet-sour sauce.

Cheese and Fruit Platter

Allow about 3 ounces of cheese per person—follow our suggestions for kinds, or choose your own. Look for cheeses imbued with herbs or wines for flavor variety. Serve cheeses on a round tray, arranging clockwise from the mildest to the strongest. Let cheeses stand at room temperature for about an hour before the party; add fruit accompaniments to the tray before serving. Arrange crackers and breads in interesting baskets.

Cheese Selection

Soft goat's cheese
Havarti or Gouda
Camembert or Brie
Stilton or blue cheese
Gorgonzola or Cambozola
Asiago or Fontina
Sharp Cheddar or Double Gloucester

Fruits

Sliced apples and pears
Red or green grapes
Dried figs, prunes and apricots

Breads

raisin-walnut, sliced baguettes
Assorted crackers

Birthday Bash

Give it a gimmicky twist to keep things fun. You can plan the party around an activity—like an athletic event for the sports nut, something raucous for the party animal or a high-roller party for the risk taker.

MENU
(serves 8)
Cocktails
Beef Stroganoff
Salad
Birthday Cake

Game Plan

It's easier than you think to go overboard and really make this kind of bash memorable. For instance, if you choose a theme, coordinate the invitations, food and decor to match, then ask your guests to dress the part. For *Oldies But Goodies*, write a catchy jingle for the invitation; play era-appropriate music; use old albums or their covers as place mats; put out props (think strobe lights and mirrored balls to evoke a disco dance hall or karaoke machines for an activity); and have someone act as DJ for the night. For a *Come As You Were* party, use a picture of the guest of honor in the invitation; blow up his or her pictures from different ages. Take digital pictures of the guests as they arrive in costume and display them on your computer monitor; have each guest retell the story of how they met the guest of honor; and play to the guest of honor's favorites (incorporate their favorite dishes, music and activities into the night). Retro comfort foods work for both of these themes.

40 Candles

2 oz. Grand Marnier

¹/₂ oz. white crème de menthe

¹/₂ oz. brandy

Cocktail; shake with ice, strain.

A Votre Santé

1 ¹/₂ oz. gin

1 oz. yellow Chartreuse

Cocktail; shake with ice, strain. Cherry garnish.

Fresh Start

1 ¹/₂ oz. Jack Daniels

¹/₂ oz. light rum

¹/₂ oz. sloe gin

Pineapple juice

Collins; pour over ice, fill with pineapple juice, stir. Cherry garnish.

Beef Stroganoff

2 pounds boneless beef sirloin steak,
cut into $1^{1}/_{2}$ x $^{1}/_{2}$-inch strips

2 tablespoons butter

2 tablespoons olive oil

4 cups sliced mushrooms

1 cup sliced onion

3 cloves garlic, minced

3 tablespoons flour

3 cups beef broth

2 teaspoons Dijon mustard

1 teaspoon dried thyme

1 cup sour cream

Salt and pepper, to taste

Chopped parsley, for garnish

6 cups cooked rice or noodles, warm

*Saute beef in butter and oil in Dutch oven until browned,
about 5 minutes; remove from pan. Add mushrooms, onion
and garlic; saute until tender, 5 to 8 minutes. Stir in
flour and cook, stirring, 1 to 2 minutes.*

*Add reserved beef, beef broth, mustard and thyme. Heat to
boiling; reduce heat and simmer, covered, until beef is tender,
20 to 30 minutes. Reduce heat to low and stir in sour cream;
cook 2 to 3 minutes. Season to taste with salt and pepper.
Transfer to chafing dish or serving bowl and sprinkle
with parsley; serve over rice.*

*Serve with crisp-tender broccoli or green beans, sprinkled with
toasted almonds, and steamed carrots sprinkled with chives.*

Salad

Arrange 8 head-lettuce wedges on a platter and sprinkle with snipped chives. Offer bowls of blue cheese and thousand island dressing for this salad with a retro past.

Tip!

Nothing has to be perfect; it's the thought that counts and the fun you have that will make the party memorable. That said, it doesn't matter if you use paper or plastic plates, but strive to do a few things that are out of the box or play to the subject's likes. If the birthday boy loves cars, decorate the place with toy versions of his favorite models. For a chocoholic or sugar addict, strew candy everywhere and ask everyone to bring an unusual sweet to serve with dessert.

Dessert

For this ageless celebration only a cake from the finest bakery will do—served with flutes of bubbly, of course! Choose a delectable layer or sheet cake, and personalize it yourself.

Look for these other fun titles from Surrey Books

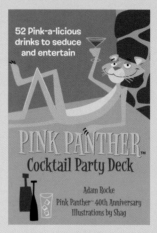

Pink Panther™ Cocktail Party Deck
ISBN 1-57284-073-0

Pink Panther™ Cocktail Party
ISBN 1-57284-072-2